J005.13
SLI

Coding Creations

Janet Slingerland

Rourke
Educational Media

rourkeeducationalmedia.com

SUPPLIES TO COMPLETE ALL PROJECTS:

This book uses Scratch, a language developed by the Lifelong Kindergarten Group at MIT Media Lab.

You Will Need:
- a computer or tablet
  - o Information on what you need to run Scratch can be found here: https://scratch.mit.edu/info/faq. Look under "What are the system requirements for Scratch?"
- access to Scratch
  - o Work with Scratch online in a browser.
  - o Download Scratch onto a computer. Go to https://scratch.mit.edu/download to get the download.
- a Scratch user account for saving and sharing projects

Other resources used or referenced in this book.
- Scratch Cards found at https://scratch.mit.edu/info/cards.
- The Scratch Creative Computing Guide found at http://scratched.gse.harvard.edu/guide.

Go to https://scratch.mit.edu/tips for instructions on Getting Started in Scratch.

Table of Contents

Getting Started

WORKING WITH SCRATCH CODE BLOCKS

Code blocks in Scratch are a lot like Legos. They are found in the *Scripts* tab for the *Stage* and sprites.

The blocks are color coded. The color of the block indicates what category the block came from. Each category has code blocks that perform functions related to that category. For instance, the Looks category contains code blocks that change the way the sprite or background looks.

Scripts	Costumes	Sounds

Motion	Events
Looks	Control
Sound	Sensing
Pen	Operators
Data	More Blocks

Blocks are coded by shape, too. Blocks are shaped so they fit together properly. When working in Scratch, you can pull the blocks apart and put them back together.

Tip:

A sprite is a computer graphic on a screen that can be moved or controlled. These are most often like characters in a story, but they can be text or other items, too.

4

CREATING A NEW PROJECT

The first step in each activity is to create a new project. You can do this one of three ways.

- Select the *Create* button, or

- Select *New Project* in My Stuff, or

- Select *File->New* while in another project

WORKING WITH SPRITES

Deleting a Sprite

A new Scratch program comes with a sprite already in it. None of the projects in this book use this sprite. To delete the sprite, do the following.

1. Click on the sprite to select it.

2. Right click on the mouse. Select delete.

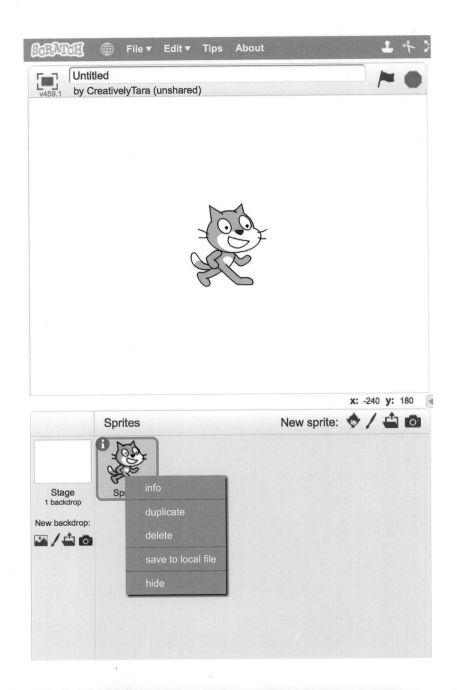

Creating a Sprite

There are several ways to create a new sprite in Scratch.

1. Select 🧑 to select a sprite from Scratch's sprite library.

2. Select ✏️ to create a sprite using the Paint Editor.

3. Select ⬆️ to bring in a sprite that has been stored as a file.

4. Select 📷 to get a picture of a sprite.

Tip: These icons are also used when creating a new costume for a sprite. Similar icons are used when creating backgrounds.

Naming a Sprite

Scratch gives each sprite a name when you create it. Here's how to change the name to something else.

1. Select the sprite.

2. Right click on the mouse. Select info.

3. Type a new name in the box.

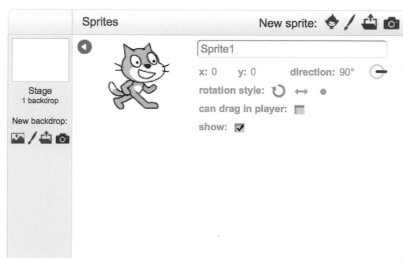

7

Waving Snowman

v459.1

Tip:

In online Scratch, add information to your project page before sharing it in the community. Add instructions on how to use your program. If you use scripts or ideas from other people, give them credit.

Create a snowman that waves when you click it and stops when you press the space bar.

Here's How:

1. Create a new project.

2. Select the *New sprite:* paintbrush icon 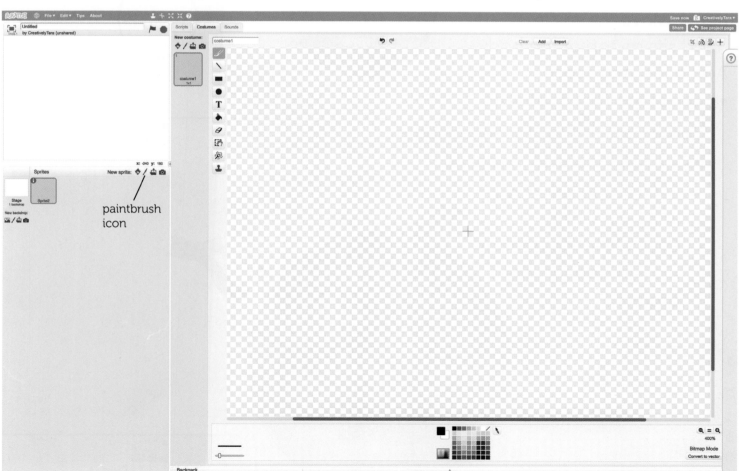 to create a new sprite.

paintbrush icon

3. Draw a snowman in the costume Paint Editor. Use *Vector Mode*, selected in the bottom right corner.

   a. Draw a large circle for the snowman's body.

   b. Draw a smaller circle for the head. Move the circles so the head sits on top of the body.

   c. Add a hat and scarf.

      • Select the *New costume*: Sprite icon 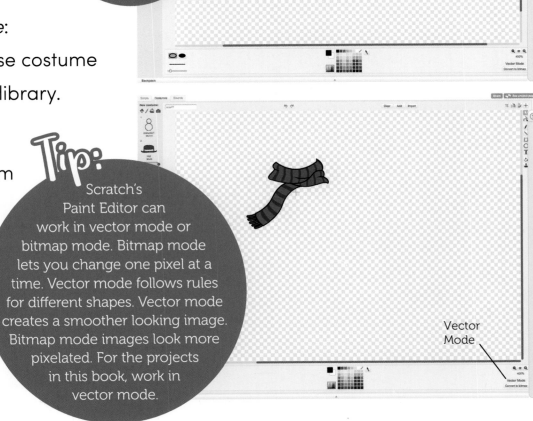 to choose costume items from the Scratch library.

         • Left click to select an item you want.

         • Click *OK* in the bottom right to add it to the project.

Tip:
To draw a circle, hold down the shift key while drawing an **ellipse**.

ellipse tool

Tip:
Scratch's Paint Editor can work in vector mode or bitmap mode. Bitmap mode lets you change one pixel at a time. Vector mode follows rules for different shapes. Vector mode creates a smoother looking image. Bitmap mode images look more pixelated. For the projects in this book, work in vector mode.

Vector Mode

d. The hat and scarf come into the project as new costumes. Move them into the screen with the snowman.

- Go into each item's costume.
- Press Ctrl + C to copy it.
- Go into the snowman costume.
- Press Ctrl + V to paste the item.
- The item shows as a ghost image. Set it in place by left clicking the mouse.

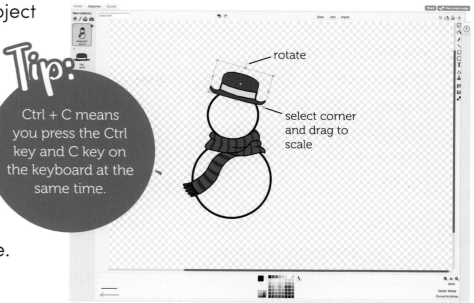

Tip!

Ctrl + C means you press the Ctrl key and C key on the keyboard at the same time.

rotate

select corner and drag to scale

e. Adjust the hat and scarf.
f. Add circle eyes and nose.
g. Use the pencil tool to draw the mouth.
h. Use the line tool to draw stick arms.
i. Color the snowman.

- Select the paint bucket to paint.
- Select a color from the **palette** or create your own color.
- Hover over the items and click to color them.

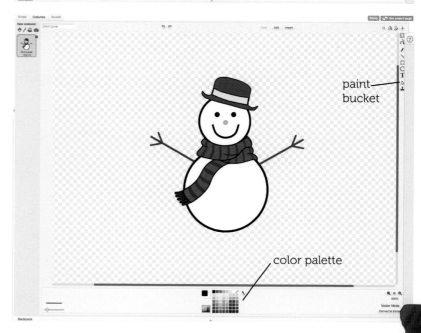

paint bucket

color palette

4. Group the lines that make up the snowman's arm. This will make it easier to **animate** the arm. Grouping objects makes multiple objects work as one. Scratch also lets you layer objects. This lets objects go in front of or behind one another.

5. Create five copies of the costume. You will use these to animate the snowman.

   a. Select the snowman costume. Right click and select duplicate.

   b. In each costume, rotate the arm slightly.

   • There should be one costume for each of these positions: up, half-up, level, half-down, and down.

group objects

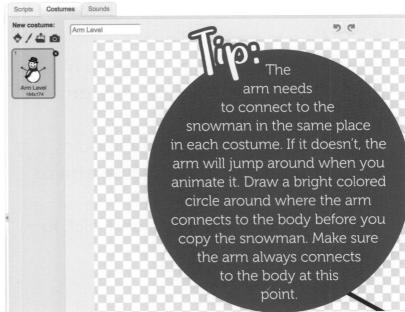

Tip: The arm needs to connect to the snowman in the same place in each costume. If it doesn't, the arm will jump around when you animate it. Draw a bright colored circle around where the arm connects to the body before you copy the snowman. Make sure the arm always connects to the body at this point.

6. Add code to make the snowman wave.

    a. Go to the snowman's *Scripts* tab.

    b. Think of the positions the snowman's arm needs to go through to wave. Add a "switch costume" block plus a "wait" block for each position.

7. Create a **variable** that will tell the snowman whether to wave or not. Select *Data*. Select *Make a Variable*. Give it a meaningful name. In the example, the variable is named *stopwave*.

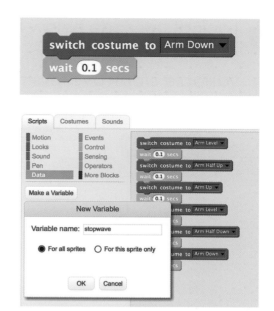

Why Does It Work?

Animation tricks the eye. It makes a set of still pictures appear to move. An image lingers in the brain for a short period of time. Switching quickly through still pictures that are slightly different makes them appear to move.

When coding animation, you need to make sure the images don't move too quickly. Computers process things faster than humans do. The wait block stops the code for that amount of time. This gives people time to see each image before it moves on to the next one.

8. Look at the code below to help you code your snowman. In this code, the snowman starts waving when it is clicked. It stops waving when the space bar is pressed. The variable *stopwave* tells the snowman whether to wave or not.

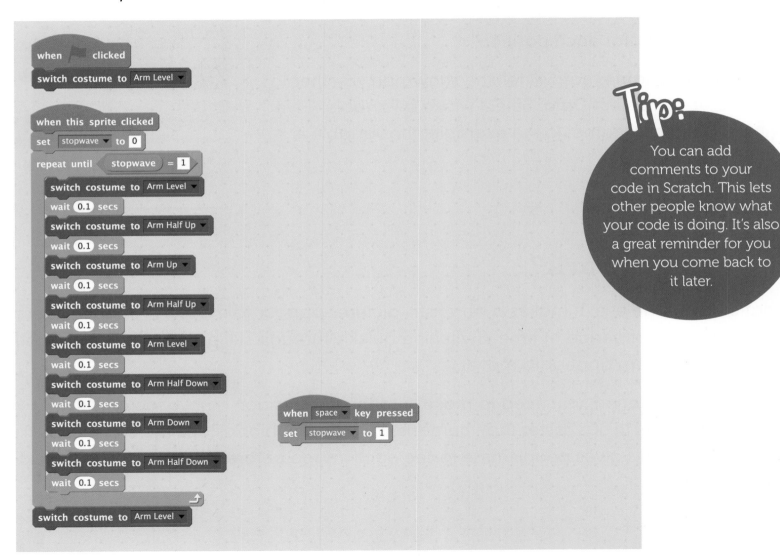

Tip:

You can add comments to your code in Scratch. This lets other people know what your code is doing. It's also a great reminder for you when you come back to it later.

Why Does It Work?

When the program starts, the computer runs through the code under  when ⚑ clicked. Events cause the other two scripts to run.

The code under when this sprite clicked starts running when the mouse clicks on the snowman. This code contains a loop, a section of code that repeats for some amount of time. This code loop has a conditional on it. It keeps running until it sees that the variable *stopwave* is set to 1.

Pressing the space bar causes the code under when space ▾ key pressed to run. This sets the *stopwave* variable to 1. The code then goes back to running the loop under when this sprite clicked. The next time the code checks *stopwave*, it will see it is set to 1 and stop running that loop.

Try This:

Delete the *stopwave* variable. Use only messages to make the snowman start and stop waving.

Musical Word

Create a word where each letter plays a different sound. The letter starts making its sound when it is clicked. It stops making the sound when it is clicked again.

Here's How:

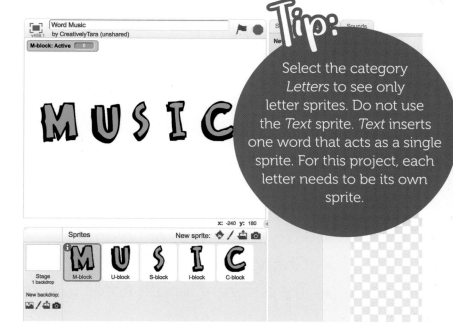

1. Create a new project.

2. Create a sprite for each letter in the word you are using. For the example shown, the word is MUSIC.

3. Use the Costume Paint Editor to color each letter.
a. Optional: create another costume to use when the letter is active, or playing its sound.

4. Arrange the letters on the *Stage* window.

5. Create a backdrop or select one from the library.

6. Decide what sound you want each letter to make. Explore all the sound options.

    a. Click on a sprite's *Sounds* tab. You can choose sounds from the library. You can record your own sounds. You can also get sounds or songs from a file. Imported files should be in MP3 or WAV format. In the project, these sounds can be selected through the "play sound" *Sound* blocks.

    b. Click on the *Scripts* tab for the sprite. Click on the *Sound* category. Explore the sound options available there. Play around with the sound until you have one (or more) you like.

        • Vary the tempo or volume.

        • Change the instrument.

        • Try different length notes and rests.

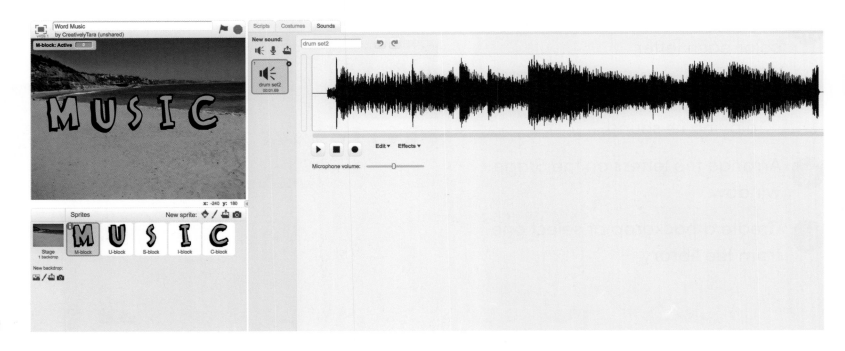

7. Create a set of scripts for each letter. In the code shown, the letter changes color and starts making music when you click it. It stops making music and changes back to its original color when you click it again. Create a variable within each letter to indicate if it is active or not. Here, it is named *Active*. Select *For This Sprite Only* to keep it within the letter.

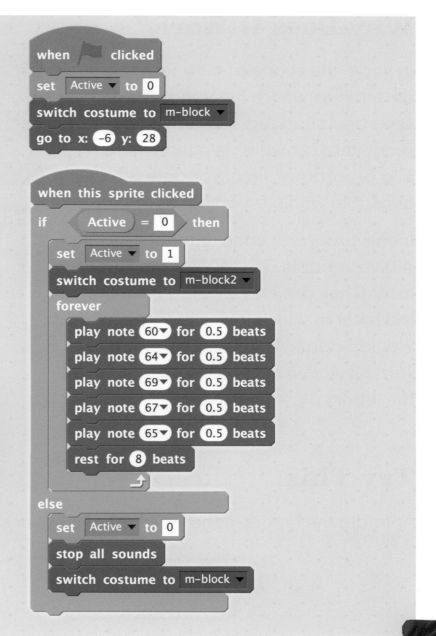

Tip:

The variable *Active* is really a Boolean variable. A Boolean has only two values. In this case, 1 and 0. A Boolean often uses the values TRUE and FALSE.

Why Does It Work?

In code, the scope of a variable determines where the variable can be seen and changed. A global variable is one that is available everywhere in a program. A local variable is only available within an object or routine.

In this program, each letter has its own *Active* variable. These variables are local. They are only available within the letter in which it was created. What would happen if *Active* was global? Turning *Active* on would make all of the letters play their sounds.

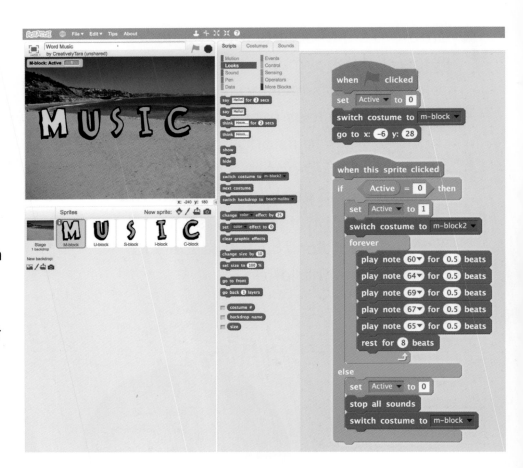

Try This:

Animate the letters in the word using suggestions in the *Animate Your Name Scratch Cards*.

Draw Square Spirals

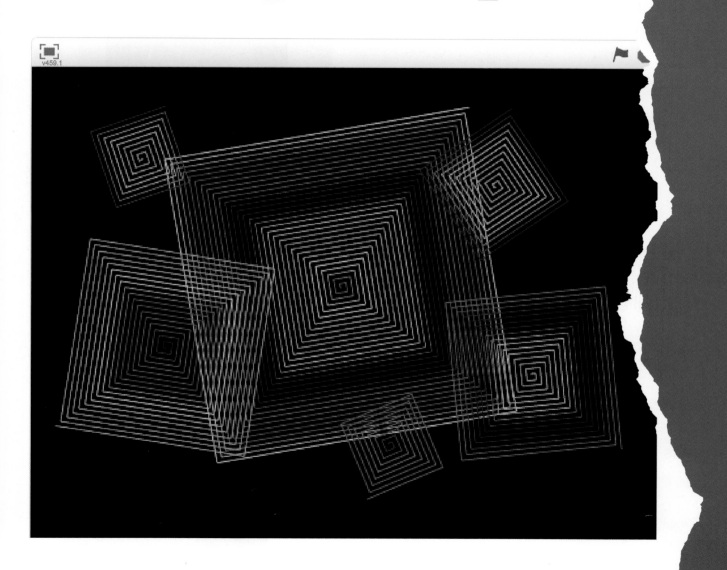

This program draws square spirals on the screen. It starts drawing wherever the mouse clicks. It starts from the center of the spiral and works out until it reaches the edge of the screen.

Here's How:

1. Create a new project.

2. Paint the backdrop black.

3. Delete the existing cat sprite.

4. Paint a new sprite in vector mode. Make it a small square or circle. In the example code, this sprite is called *drawingpen*.

5. Add code to start drawing when the mouse clicks on the screen. This code goes on the *Scripts* area for the *Backdrop*. It broadcasts a message named "draw" when the *Stage* is clicked.

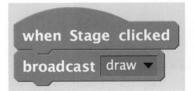

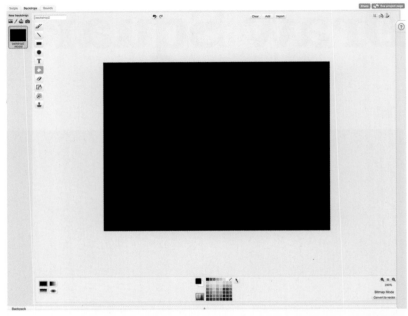

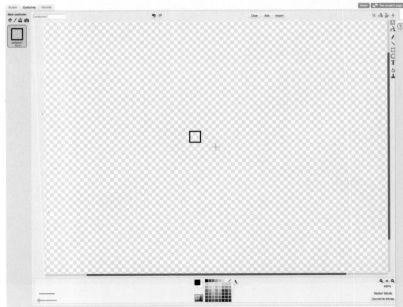

6. Go to the *Scripts* area for the sprite *drawingpen*. Add the code shown below.

Tip:

The pen can draw in any direction. It points in a direction based on the degrees of a circle.

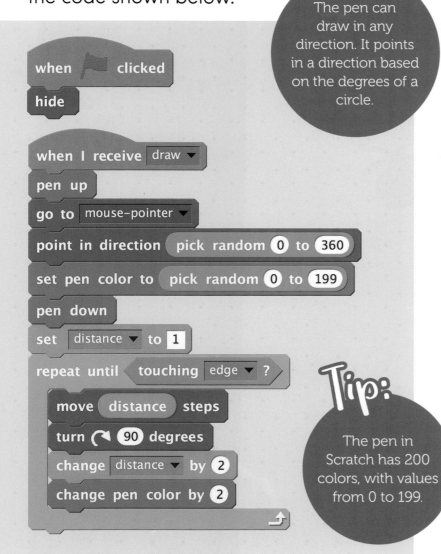

```
when [flag] clicked
hide

when I receive [draw ▼]
pen up
go to [mouse-pointer ▼]
point in direction (pick random (0) to (360))
set pen color to (pick random (0) to (199))
pen down
set [distance ▼] to (1)
repeat until < touching [edge ▼] ? >
    move (distance) steps
    turn ↻ (90) degrees
    change [distance ▼] by (2)
    change pen color by (2)
```

Tip:

The pen in Scratch has 200 colors, with values from 0 to 199.

Why Does It Work?

A square is a shape with four equal sides. All four corners have interior angles equal to 90 degrees. To draw a square, the pen would draw a set distance and turn 90 degrees four times. To draw a square spiral, the size of each side must increase slightly from the side before it.

Try This:

- Code the pen to draw a square.
- Change the turn to something other than 90 degrees.
- Make rectangular spirals.
  - Change the size of the *drawingpen* sprite.

23

Flying Helicopter Game

YOU WILL NEED:

The *Make It Fly* cards from the set of *Scratch Cards* found here: scratch.mit.edu/info/cards

Tip: Test your code frequently as you are developing it. Try out and debug each capability as you add it.

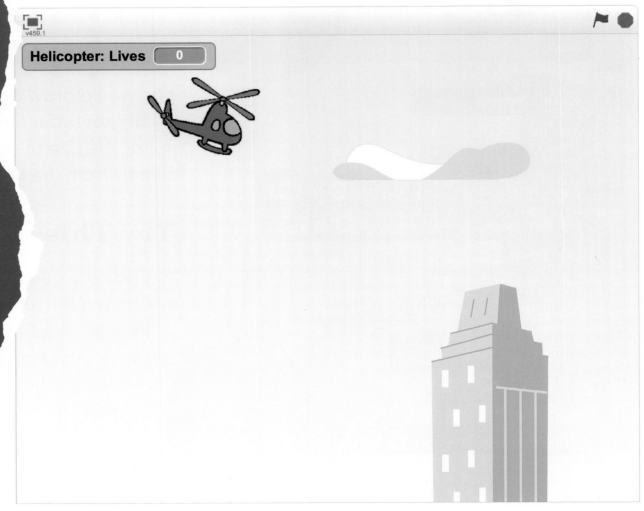

Helicopter: Lives   0

Code a game where a helicopter flies through a city. The player uses the arrow keys to move around objects. The player wins when it dodges all objects for some amount of time.

Here's How:

1. Create a new project.

2. Follow the instructions on the first five *Make It Fly* cards.

    a. On Card 1, choose the *Helicopter* sprite.

    b. The code in Cards 2 and 3 go on the *Buildings* sprite.

    c. The code in Card 4 goes on the *Helicopter* sprite.

    d. On Card 5, be sure to pick the *Clouds*, not the *Cloud*, sprite. Change the "pick **random** block" to pick a number between –90 and 180.

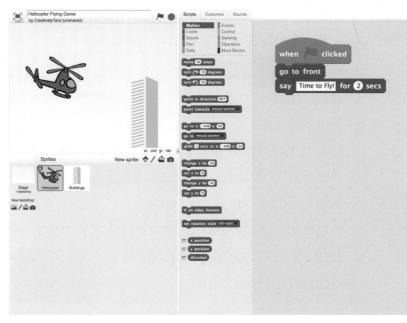

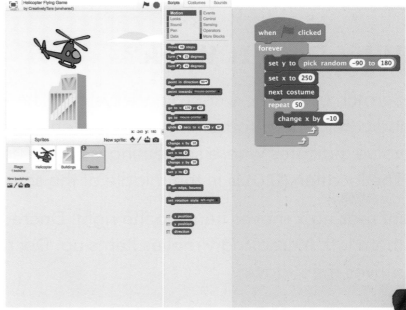

3. Change the helicopter to make it smaller. **Simulate** gravity so it is constantly falling.

   a. Add `set size to 50 %` from *Looks* to the start of the program to make the helicopter smaller.

   b. Pick a place where you would like the helicopter to start the game. Move it there on the *Stage* window. Add the *Motion* block `go to x: -95 y: 89` to put the helicopter in that spot.

   c. Add a "forever" *Control* block and *Motion* y-axis block so the helicopter is constantly falling.

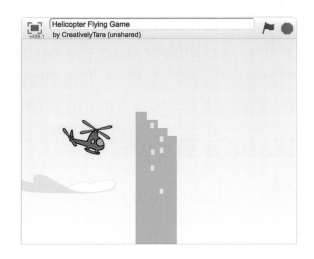

Why Does It Work?

Scratch uses an x-y coordinate system. The x value indicates where something is on the left-right axis. The y value indicates where something is on the up-down axis. The location (0,0) is in the middle of the screen.

Increasing x moves items to the right. Decreasing x moves them left. Increasing y moves items up. Decreasing y moves them down.

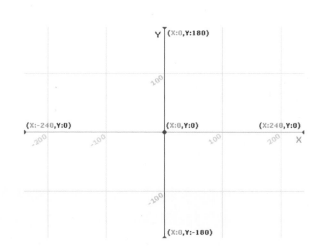

4. Decide how many lives the player will get. Add code so the player loses a life if the helicopter hits a building.

   a. In *Data*, add a variable called *Lives*.

   b. Add a code block to the beginning of the game to set *Lives* to the maximum number of lives. Use . Change 0 to the number of lives you've chosen.

   c. Add code to the "forever loop" to check if the helicopter is touching a building. If so, make a pop sound and lose a life.

   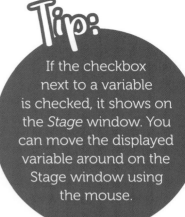

   d. Check if all lives have been lost.
   - If so, stop the game. Add a sound effect and text telling the player they've lost the game.
   - If there are still lives left, go back to the starting position.

Tip!
If the checkbox next to a variable is checked, it shows on the *Stage* window. You can move the displayed variable around on the Stage window using the mouse.

Why Does It Work?

This program uses many conditional statements. A conditional is a portion of code that only runs if some condition is met. In an IF statement, the code inside that block runs if the condition is met. If the conditions are not met, the computer skips that code and continues on. An IF statement may have an ELSE. If the IF condition is not met, the computer runs the portion of code in the ELSE section. IF statements can be nested as they are in this program.

5. Decide how long the player needs to fly the helicopter without hitting something to win the game. Add code to use the Scratch timer to decide if the player won.

a. Add the `reset timer` *Sensing* code block to the beginning and when resetting after losing a life.

b. Add a check if the timer is above the time needed to win. The timer counts in seconds. In this code segment, the time to win is 2 minutes or 120 seconds.

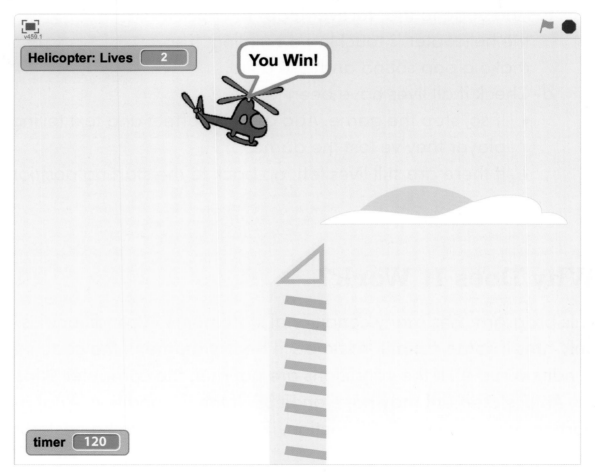

6. Your code should look something like this:

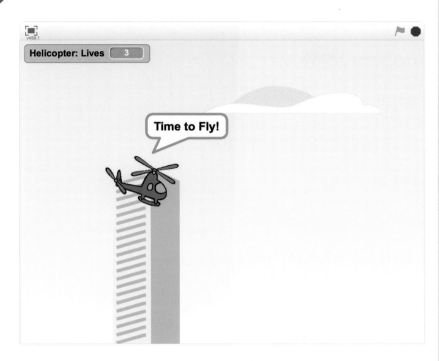

Try This:

- Add flying objects to dodge or catch.

- Change the object of the game. The player wins when they collect a certain number of objects. (Refer to *Make It Fly* cards 6 and 7.)

```
when 🏳 clicked
go to front
set Lives to 3
say Time to Fly! for 2 secs
set size to 50 %
go to x: -95 y: 89
reset timer
forever
    change y by -1
    if touching Buildings ? then
        play sound pop
        change Lives by -1
        if Lives = 0 then
            say Sorry, You Lose! for 2 secs
            play sound gong until done
            stop all
        else
            go to x: -95 y: 89
            reset timer
    if timer > 120 then
        play sound cheer until done
        say You Win! for 2 secs
        stop all
```

Glossary

animate (AN-ih-mayt): to make something appear to move

ellipse (eh-LIPS): a shape that looks like a flattened circle

palette (PAL-eht): the range of colors used in a painting or design

random (RAN-dum): showing no clear pattern or plan

simulate (SIHM-you-layt): to mimic or act like something else

variable (VAR-ee-ah-buhl): something that can take on different values

Index

Show What You Know

1. Describe how to animate a picture.

2. What is an event?

3. Describe how a conditional works.

4. What does a loop do?

5. What is the difference between a local and a global variable?

Further Reading

Bedell, Jane (J.M.), *So You Want to be a Coder? The Ultimate Guide to a Career in Programming, VideoGame Creation, Robotics and More!*, Aladdin, 2016.

Scott, Marc, *A Beginner's Guide to Coding*, Bloomsbury, 2017.

Woodcock, Jon, *Coding Games in Scratch*, DK, 2015.

About the Author

Before writing books for children, Janet Slingerland wrote code. She spent 15 years programming computers in things like submarines, telephones, and airplanes. Janet lives in New Jersey with her husband, three children, and a dog.

Meet The Author!
www.meetREMauthors.com

www.rourkeeducationalmedia.com

PHOTO CREDITS: Cover & all pages: © creativelytara; All screenshots by "Scratch is developed by the Lifelong Kindergarten Group at the MIT Media Lab. It is available for free at https://scratch.mit.edu".

Edited by: Keli Sipperley
Cover and Interior design by: Tara Raymo • CreativelyTara • www.creativelytara.com

Library of Congress PCN Data

Coding Creations / Janet Slingerland
(Make It!)
ISBN 978-1-64156-440-3 (hard cover)
ISBN 978-1-64156-566-0 (soft cover)
ISBN 978-1-64156-685-8 (e-Book)
Library of Congress Control Number: 2018930468

Rourke Educational Media
Printed in the United States of America,
North Mankato, Minnesota